by Ellen Brammar

Modest was first performed at Hull Truck Theatre
on 23 May 2023, before touring to Crucible Theatre,
Sheffield; Northern Stage, Newcastle; New Wolsey Theatre,
Ipswich; Stephen Joseph Theatre, Scarborough; The
Warehouse in Holbeck, Leeds; and Kiln Theatre, London.

Elizabeth	Emer Dineen
Alice/RA Two	Fizz Sinclair
RA One/Mary	LJ Parkinson
RA Three/Frances	Isabel Adomakoh Young
Millais/Cora/Aide	Jacqui Bardelang
Bessie/Queen Vic	Libra Teejay

Creative and Production Team

Writer	Ellen Brammar
Composer and Musical Director	Rachel Barnes
Co-Director	Luke Skilbeck
Co-Director	Paul Smith
Assistant Director	Prime Isaac
Set Designer	QianEr Jin
Costume Designer	Terry Herfield
Associate Costume Designer	Siân Thomas
Lighting Designer	Jessie Addinall
Sound Designer and Music Producer	Eliyana Evans
Movement Director	Tamar Draper & Jo Ashbridge for Tamar and Jo Dance Company
Dramaturg	Matthew May
Producer	Bellaray Bertrand-Webb
Production Manager	Emily Anderton
Sound Engineer	Tom Smith
Stage Manager	Jay Hirst
Deputy Stage Manager	Danielle Harris

Company Stage Manager	Shona Wright
Sensitivity Reader	mandla
Engagement Coordinators	Same Circle Theatre
BSL Interpreter (Hull)	Rose Priestley

Modest is a Middle Child production in collaboration with Milk Presents. It is funded by Arts Council England and Hull City Council and was developed with the support of the National Theatre's Generate programme.

MIDDLE CHILD

Middle Child are a Hull-based company creating gig theatre that brings people together for a good night out with big ideas. We tell untold stories which capture the electrifying moment when the beat drops, mixing original live music with bold new writing. Our events are live and loud, making sense of the modern world.

We are committed to breaking down barriers and ensuring that theatre is affordable and accessible for all. We will set fire to your expectations of what a night at the theatre can be.

Our artist development programme ensures that artists in Hull are given top-class development opportunities across disciplines, without having to leave the city.

We are an Arts Council England National Portfolio Organisation and an associate company of Paines Plough, supported by Hull City Council.

'There is a disconnect between an industry predominantly based in metropolitan areas and those who feel unheard, those who never go to the theatre, who think it's not for them, or who have no access. Middle Child is the kind of company that can bridge the gap.' Lyn Gardner in *The Stage*

Middle Child are:

Artistic Director and CEO	Paul Smith
Finance and Operations Manager	Emily Anderton
Audience Development Manager	Jamie Potter
Senior Producer	Sarah Penney
Assistant Producer	Erin Anderson
Literary Manager	Matthew May

Founding Company Members

Mungo Beaumont, Ellen Brammar, Emma Bright, Sophie Clay, Edward Cole, Marc Graham and James Townsend.

Trustees

Amanda Smethurst (chair), Jane Fallowfield, Jack Heaton, Rozzy Knox, Jay Mitra, Magda Moses, Chris Tonge, Emma Tucker and John R. Wilkinson.

Middle Child Mates

Middle Child's work is made possible by our pay what you can supporters' scheme, Middle Child Mates. Sign up today at middlechildtheatre.co.uk/mates

Middle Child is a company limited by guarantee and a charity. Registered company number: 09921306. Charity number: 1188756.

Middle Child
42-43 High Street Hull HU1 1PS
+44 (0)1482 221857
middlechildtheatre.co.uk

Follow @middlechildhull on Twitter, Facebook and Instagram.

Milk Presents celebrate queer bodies, uplift queer stories and centre creativity, resilience, action and joy.

Our mission is to improve the lives of trans and queer people, to build a world where queer and trans people are valued, fulfilled and respected and where LGBTQIA+ histories, stories and bodies are visible and celebrated. We do this through performance, club nights, theatre, cabaret, drag, installation and film.

Founded in 2010, Milk Presents are at the forefront of queer performance, touring queer work throughout the UK and internationally. The company are previous associates of Derby Theatre and the Bush Theatre.

Milk Presents have created numerous shows including *JOAN* (Winner of Off-West End Award and Edinburgh Fringe First Award), *Bluebeard a Fairytale for Adults*, *Bullish*, *Self Service*, *Marty and The Party* (Derby Theatre), *The Bear/ The Proposal* (Young Vic) and *Trans Filth and Joy* (made with Trans Creative and Manchester Pride).

Milk Presents
Luke Skilbeck
Ruby Glaskin
Adam Robertson
Jo Tyabji
Prime Isaac
Lee Smith

MODEST

Ellen Brammar

For my bossy people, A & K,
be wonderful, brilliant you.

Characters

ELIZABETH, *twenty-six. Artist, exceptionally talented. Self-assured*

ALICE, *twenty-five, trans woman. Poet, exceptionally talented. Activist, Elizabeth's sister*

BESSIE, *sixteen, non-binary. Budding artist. Working class. Huge fan of Elizabeth*

FRANCES, *twenty-six, Black. Artist, suffragist, activist, intelligent*

MARY, *twenty-seven. Artist, queer, kind-hearted*

CORA, *twenty-five. Artist. A fine painter. A little naive and unworldly*

RA ONE, *fifty-five. Artist and president of Royal Academy. Pompous, ruthless*

RA TWO, *sixty-five. Artist. Misogynist*

RA THREE, *twenty-six. Artist. Ignorant and easily swayed*

MILLAIS, *forty-five. Artist. Liberal by 1870s standards*

HANGING COMMITTEE, *forty. Artist. Officious and a stickler for details*

AIDE, *thirty. Diligent and eager to please*

QUEEN VIC, *fifty-five. A woman at the top*

Race and gender of characters is open, unless stated otherwise. Ages are from the start of the play in 1874.

Suggested Doubling

ALICE and RA TWO

RA ONE and MARY

MILLAIS, AIDE and CORA

HANGING COMMITTEE, RA THREE and FRANCES

BESSIE and QUEEN VIC

Notes

The play takes place from 1874 to 1879.

A forward slash (/) indicates an interruption.

Words in square brackets [ ] can be unspoken or half-spoken.

Scene Title References

'I would have girls regard themselves not as adjectives but as nouns.' – Elizabeth Cady Stanton

'The true man wants two things: danger and play. For that reason he wants woman, as the most dangerous plaything.' – Friedrich Nietzsche

'Babes Never Die' – Honeyblood

'They call it art. Maybe.' – *Standing Female Nude*, Carol Ann Duffy

'My love is political. My body is political. I talk even when I don't speak.' – Indya Moore

'Pressure is a privilege – it only comes to those who earn it.' – Billie Jean King

'Have a big crazy dream and see where it takes you.' – Maggie Aderin-Pocock

'The truth will set you free, but first it will piss you off.' – Gloria Steinem

'I can see the Queen of England gazing on my shape. Magnificent, she murmurs, moving on.' – *Standing Female Nude*, Carol Ann Duffy

'Gotta blame it on my juice.' – Lizzo

'Hope is a very unruly emotion.' – Gloria Steinem

'I just love bossy women.' – Amy Poehler

'These artists take themselves too seriously.' – *Standing Female Nude*, Carol Ann Duffy

'A place you can live out a fantasy you have never lived before.' – Michaela Jaé Rodriguez

'You are the problem here.' – First Aid Kit

'A woman without a man is like a fish without a bicycle.' – Gloria Steinem

'I'm a woman, phenomenally. Phenomenal woman, that's me.' – *Phenomenal Woman*, Maya Angelou

This text went to press before the end of rehearsals and so may differ slightly from the play as performed.

ACT ONE

ONE – IT'S ALL TRUE. APART FROM WHEN WE'RE LYING

We are at Burlington House. The RAS (ROYAL ACADEMICIANS) *are already on stage. They might be painting an audience member, inspecting the art, chatting together.* RA ONE *steps forward, he addresses the room of hopeful artists,* RA THREE *follows closely behind. (The following speech should be full of liveness and fun.)*

RA ONE. Welcome. Sit. (*Etc.*) Let me extend our warmest welcome to you all. You hopeful artists.

RA THREE. Aren't you lucky to be here tonight? Getting to glimpse behind the curtain, into my world.

RA ONE. Our world. The world of art. There is no finer place. And to think, you could become a part of it.

RA THREE. The commonest of man.

RA ONE. For the Summer Exhibition is open to anyone. If your work is good enough then we will hang it. Here. Right here alongside mine.

RA THREE. And mine.

RA ONE. And theirs. It is quite a thing, is it not? Of course, your art is unlikely to be hung right next to mine.

RA THREE. Yes, or mine.

RA ONE. The RAs' work, being of a higher calibre, will be hung on the line, it is only fair that the public see the finest work at eye level. We don't want the ladies cricking their elegant swan necks trying to find my work up high. No, we find it best if the unknown artists take the skied spots.

RA THREE. It is only fair.

ELIZABETH *enters, she is here as a 'hopeful artist' too. She takes up space and is fucking marvellous. She should literally sparkle.*

RA ONE. Now. Welcome to the Royal Academy of Arts.

ELIZABETH *smiles.*

TWO – 'I WOULD HAVE GIRLS REGARD THEMSELVES NOT AS ADJECTIVES BUT AS NOUNS'

It's 1874. We are in ELIZABETH*'s family home, it is grand, like her. She is painting, confidence emanates from her. She sings as she paints.*

Song: 'A Talent Like Me'

ELIZABETH.
> *I've never seen one like me before.*
> *I've never seen one like me.*
> *Where my talent will make you scream for more*
> *Honey, just you wait and see*
> *(Just you wait and see.)*
>
> *I'm just that good, there's no hiding away*
> *If you've got it, gotta let it shine*
> *And I'm the one that's got it huge*
> *There is no talent like this talent of mine.*
>
> *Oh yes, they're in for a right treat here*
> *My paintings are one of a kind*
> *Bet they'd never imagined it'd be this good*
> *I promise this is going to blow their fucking minds.*
>
> *'Cause they've never seen one like me before.*
> *They've never seen one like me.*
> *My talent will open all their locked doors*
> *I'm wonderful and they'll see*
> *They will see me.*

ALICE *enters*.

ALICE. When do you leave?

ELIZABETH. Soon.

ALICE. Are you okay?

ELIZABETH. Yes.

ALICE. You are nervous.

ELIZABETH. No.

ALICE. Oh, please.

ELIZABETH. I am not. It's an excellent painting. I am an exceptional artist. (*Pause while she waits for* ALICE *to agree*.) You do agree? It is an excellent painting?

ALICE. Yes.

ELIZABETH. It's an excellent / painting...

ALICE. It's an excellent painting.

ELIZABETH (*beat*). What's wrong? Tell me, I can take it.

ALICE. Not everything is about you, Mimi.

ELIZABETH. Since when? What then? What is it?

ALICE. [It's just] stubble. I can feel it growing in.

ELIZABETH. You can hardly see it.

ALICE. I can feel it.

ELIZABETH. Alice, it's fine. It's not / even noticeable.

ALICE. It is not fine.

ELIZABETH. You are beautiful, as always, Alice. It doesn't make you any less of a / [woman]

ALICE. Please, I don't want to talk about it.

ELIZABETH. Okay, that's fine. (*Pause*.) So you do think it's an excellent painting then?

ALICE. It's an excellent painting. Your best.

ELIZABETH. Exactly. I knew it, no need for nerves.

ALICE. Your confidence is startling, Mimi.

ELIZABETH. You think me arrogant?

ALICE. No. (*Beat.*) Others might.

ELIZABETH. No man would dare suggest such a thing. It would be unchivalrous, tantamount to impugning my femininity.

ALICE. And if it didn't come from a man?

ELIZABETH. No one would listen.

They laugh.

Besides, it has been accepted.

ALICE. Yes.

ELIZABETH. And it is an exceptional painting.

ALICE. Truly exceptional.

ELIZABETH. Therefore it will be hung in a favourable position.

ALICE. I do not doubt it.

ELIZABETH (*beat*). Oh shit, what if it is skied? I do not think I could take the humiliation.

ALICE. Again.

ELIZABETH. Yes, again. Thank you. I thought my neck would never stand straight again after the last time.

ALICE. I will buy you a brace.

Pause.

It will not be skied.

ELIZABETH. No?

ALICE. Fourth time lucky.

ELIZABETH. I'm nervous.

ALICE. Yes, I know.

ELIZABETH. No, you don't.

ALICE. Yes I do.

ELIZABETH. Only because I just told you.

ALICE. You are impossible.

ELIZABETH. Yes. Of course. I am an artist.

THREE – OH, BUT SHE'S SO PRETTY

ELIZABETH *arrives at Burlington House for Varnishing Day. Artists are climbing over each other to varnish their paintings. Everyone is trying to get a good look at each other's work.*

HANGING COMMITTEE. Name?

ELIZABETH. Miss Thompson.

HANGING COMMITTEE. Miss Elizabeth Thompson?

ELIZABETH. Yes.

HANGING COMMITTEE. You are the artist who painted *Calling the Roll After an Engagement, Crimea*?

ELIZABETH. Yes.

HANGING COMMITTEE. The painting with the dimensions thirty-six-point-seven by seventy-two-point-two inches?

ELIZABETH. Yes.

HANGING COMMITTEE. An artwork in which you depict The Grenadier Guards in Crimea, oil-on-canvas?

ELIZABETH. For fuck sake. Yes.

HANGING COMMITTEE. But you are so pretty.

ELIZABETH. Yes.

HANGING COMMITTEE. Goodness. Right, well. Gallery Two.

ELIZABETH What?

HANGING COMMITTEE. Gallery Two.

ELIZABETH. Are you being serious?

HANGING COMMITTEE. Always.

ELIZABETH. Fuck.

HANGING COMMITTEE. You are in for a greater surprise then that, Miss Thompson.

ELIZABETH. What do you mean?

HANGING COMMITTEE. Let me show you.

ELIZABETH *walks into Gallery Two to see her painting hanging ON THE LINE. This should be a huge deal.*

There.

ELIZABETH. It is on the line.

HANGING COMMITTEE. I know.

ELIZABETH. My painting.

HANGING COMMITTEE. Yes.

ELIZABETH. My Grenadiers.

HANGING COMMITTEE. Marvellous.

ELIZABETH. My Dark Battalion.

HANGING COMMITTEE. Sexy.

ELIZABETH. Hanging on the fucking line.

HANGING COMMITTEE. Congratulations, my dear. What a thing. A woman. On the line in Gallery Two of all places. I never thought I'd see the day. This is progress, my dear.

Long overdue, but we mustn't grumble because here you are. Now off you go, have fun. Varnishing day is to be enjoyed, especially if you happen to be one of the most talented artists here. Go.

ELIZABETH *hurries away to join the other artists to varnish* The Roll Call.

Gosh. So pretty.

FOUR – 'THE TRUE MAN WANTS TWO THINGS: DANGER AND PLAY. FOR THAT REASON HE WANTS WOMAN, AS THE MOST DANGEROUS PLAYTHING'

The RAS *enter. They are 'The Forty'.*

Song: 'Chops to Feet'

THE RAS.
> *We are men*
> *Yes we are*
> *The finest men*
> *We set the bar*
> *The most gentlemen-y men*
> *You will ever meet*
> *Arty and stylish*
> *From mutton chops to feet.*

RA ONE *reads a review from* The Daily Telegraph.

RA ONE.... 'real genius has no insurmountable obstacles to encounter from "The Forty."'

RA TWO. Quite right.

RA ONE. Ah, yes, and here, here, yes, 'A liberal institution'.

MILLAIS. They actually call us that?

RA ONE. They do.

MILLAIS. Liberal.   RA TWO. Oh god.

RA ONE. I know. Gush, gush, gush... 'one so young'... 'a woman'...

RA TWO. How old is she exactly? Obviously very young. And barely a woman really. In the proper way that women are women.

MILLAIS. Which is what?

RA TWO. Cheeky.

RA THREE. She is twenty-three, The Prince of Wales said so at the banquet. So young.

RA ONE. He was given the wrong information.

MILLAIS. Yes, she is twenty-six.

RA ONE. Still young though.

RA TWO. And very pretty.

RA THREE. It's strange, isn't it, that a woman so young / who is so pretty and so delicate...

MILLAIS. She is the same age as you.

RA THREE. Yes, but I am a man and she is a delicate female flower.

RA TWO. Just a little girly really.

RA THREE. Yes, and yet she has painted something so manly.

RA ONE. They are a veritable band of brothers, are they not? Quite magnificent.

MILLAIS. It is an embodiment of masculinity, no question. But look at the skill, she is immeasurably talented. I mean, for goodness' sake, it could have been painted by a man.

RA TWO. Yes, yes, it is wonderful, but how did she come to paint such a subject?

RA ONE. It is quite a leap from fruit and flowers.

RA TWO. Perhaps she has been tutored in the art of the unveiled man / like a dirty whore?

RA THREE. Do you think? Golly.

MILLAIS. I doubt it.

RA ONE. They have an air of us about them, don't you think?

RA THREE. Yes, I do think.

RA TWO. Men.

RA THREE. Lads. Lads, lads, lads.

RA ONE. So manly and yet so sensitive. Liberal, I suppose.

MILLAIS. Liberal? Yes. Liberal men.

RA ONE. It's truly remarkable.

MILLAIS. A bunch of liberal men. How fantastic.

FIVE – 'BABES NEVER DIE'

ELIZABETH *bursts into her home*. ALICE *is sitting quietly writing*.

ELIZABETH. Alice. Alice. Where are you?

ALICE. Right here. Do not shout.

ELIZABETH. Well?

ALICE. What?

ELIZABETH. Ask me. Come on, hurry up.

ALICE. I am just / finishing this [poem]

ELIZABETH. You are being slow on purpose.

ALICE. I was about to ask.

ELIZABETH. Do it then.

ALICE (*being deliberately slow*). Where?

ELIZABETH. Gallery Two.

ALICE. No?

ELIZABETH. On the line.

ALICE. That's... goodness, I cannot quite believe it.

ELIZABETH (*incredulous*). You cannot quite believe it?

ALICE. No, I mean... (*Beat.*) I am so pleased for you, Mimi.

ELIZABETH. I am pleased for me too. Immensely. It was wonderful. I was wonderful. Everyone was shaking my hand and telling me what an accomplished work it is. And it looks beautiful, hanging smack bang in front of your eyes. It's going to be huge, Alice. I think this could be the start for me. There was talk of my election.

ALICE. Your election?

ELIZABETH. Into the academy.

ALICE. Really?

ELIZABETH. Yes. What?

ALICE. That seems a bit, I don't know, are you sure?

ELIZABETH. Yes.

ALICE. Maybe they were being nice?

ELIZABETH. Maybe they were being serious?

ALICE. Mimi.

ELIZABETH. Why not? Give me a reason.

ALICE. I can think of two fairly obvious ones.

   ALICE *nods towards* ELIZABETH*'s boobs.*

ELIZABETH. Victoria and Albert? No, I don't believe that.

ALICE. There has never been a woman elected into the academy.

ELIZABETH. Until now.

ALICE. You would have to be astonishingly fortunate.

ELIZABETH. Or simply astonishing.

ALICE. Are you serious?

ELIZABETH. Yes.

ALICE. You think they are just going to let you in?

ELIZABETH. Of course. I am no ordinary woman. I am these
    men's contemporary, their better in most cases. Alice, I have
    painted a picture that has been hung in the most favourable
    of positions. I'm a bloody star in that place. You should
    have seen the other artists, they were jealous, I could see it,
    dripping off of their sweaty pig faces. It was delightful.

ALICE. Elizabeth, yes, you have talent / but

ELIZABETH. I exude talent.

ALICE. But, we know dozens of accomplished women, and
    not one has made it to the heights that you are dreaming of. I
    just do not think it can be done. I do not think they will let it
    happen.

ELIZABETH. I will single myself out.

ALICE. I do not doubt that. But I worry that you will be hurt, I
    am not sure you can win.

ELIZABETH. Yes, I can. I will. You just wait, Alice. This time
    next year I will be a Royal Academician. Miss Elizabeth
    Thompson, RA.

    Song: 'Modest'

ELIZABETH.
    A woman should be modest in her talent
    Especially around a man
    You have to make them think that they are gallant
    For paying you attention in any way
    A girl must not admit to her magnificence
    She must plead ignorant and dumb

And that might make her seem a trifle dense
But a man needs to feel smarter than you

I am young
I am pretty
I am sweet
And oh so disgustingly talented
But best of all
Most importantly
I am modest

A woman should be modest in her talents
Especially around a man
Oh so careful not to tip the balance
Making sure he always feels in control
A star, like me, should always be modest
Men need your face to show surprise
Who me? A work of art? A goddess?
You are too kind, sir. I'm not. I'm just me

I'm the best
I'm a star
I'm a goddess
I paint with the skill of ten men (or more)
But best of all
Most importantly
This is the thing I know
I will win because
I am modest.

SIX – THE ART OF FLATTERY

ELIZABETH *is at the academy admiring her picture.* RA ONE *approaches her from behind, giving her waist a little nip.*

RA ONE. Roll Call Thompson.

ELIZABETH. Sorry?

RA ONE. It is what they are calling you.

ELIZABETH. Oh.

RA ONE. And there it is.

ELIZABETH. Yes.

RA ONE. Magnificent.

ELIZABETH. Yes. But, no, you are too kind, sir.

RA ONE. You must be pleased.

ELIZABETH. Absolutely. Although, a touch overwhelmed too.

RA ONE. Overwhelmed?

ELIZABETH. By the academy's kindness.

RA ONE. Nonsense, this is all down to you, my dear.

ELIZABETH. There you go again. You have a generous spirit.

RA ONE. Well...

ELIZABETH. You must hear that a great deal.

RA ONE. On occasion.

ELIZABETH. I want to thank you, sir, the academy, for your generosity.

RA ONE. It was not generosity, Miss Thompson. The academy recognises talent and rewards it accordingly.

ELIZABETH. Of course, I do not doubt it.

RA ONE. The academy is open to all, despite what you may have heard.

ELIZABETH. I have heard nothing. I do not subscribe to gossip.

RA ONE. I am glad to hear it.

ELIZABETH. And, if I had heard things, which I have not, I would not dream of believing them.

RA ONE. Good. It is refreshing to hear of such loyalty.

ELIZABETH. I am the academy's woman. Through and
through. Haven't you heard?

RA ONE. The academy's woman? What a pleasant turn of
phrase.

ELIZABETH. I couldn't agree more.

RA ONE. Fabulous.

ELIZABETH (*to herself*). Yes. I am, aren't I?

SEVEN – BESSIE

BESSIE (*sixteen*) *clutches a clipping of a photograph cut from
the paper. They speak directly to the audience.*

BESSIE. Dear Miss Thompson. My name is Bessie. You might
think I'm a girl, I'm not. I'm not a boy either. I'm Bessie.
Artist in the making. And I'm your biggest fan. That's me.
Y'see I know your painting off by heart. You can test me if
you want, if we ever meet. My favourite bit is that soldier at
the front, who's collapsed. Dead, I think. I'll be able to tell
properly when I see it in colour, up close and right there. I
know you'll have done something to his skin. Some detail.
You are wonderful like that. When I'm an artist I'll be really
good at details too. Ma says that it will never happen. That I
can dream about it all I want but that don't make it so. I think
she's wrong, don't you? I used to dream about being Bessie,
and I made that happen. Well, sort of, for some of the time,
not all of the time, but that's who I am. And that's what you
know me as too. I like that. (*Beat.*) My next favourite bit,
well actually I really hate him, is that okay to say? I'm sure
you would have wanted that. It's the soldier that's surrounded
by all the men, his friends, all slumped and sad and
exhausted and he's there, standing to attention. Proper little
lickspittle. So I like it but I hate it too. Which is why you're
so incredible. You make it complicated. It's like, it's like you

can feel it. Feel the pain. The dirt. The blood. The bile. Like
you're there with them. Dying with them. That's what I've
heard, anyway. I haven't actually been yet, only seen it in the
paper. But I'm saving up. It's taking ages but I'm doing it.
All by myself too. It's a bob to get in, did you know that? If
Ma knew she'd kill me. But I know it'll be worth it. I will see
it. I'm gonna be a part of it. (*Beat*.) Imagine if I meet you. Oh
friggedy farthing, I think I'd combust.

EIGHT – 'THEY CALL IT ART. MAYBE'

The actor playing BESSIE *changes into* QUEEN VIC, *suddenly
they demand attention.* QUEEN VIC *is in Buckingham Palace
and is accompanied by her* AIDE.

QUEEN VIC. What is it called?

AIDE. *Calling the Roll After an Engagement, Crimea.*

QUEEN VIC. Catchy.

AIDE. Yes, Ma'am.

QUEEN VIC. And the people like it?

AIDE. They adore it, Ma'am.

QUEEN VIC. I want to see it.

AIDE. Yes, Ma'am.

> *The* AIDE *exits.* QUEEN VIC *stares out and waits with all
> the patience of someone who does not often have to wait.*
> AIDE *rushes back and gestures out to the audience. The
> audience is now* The Roll Call.

> Your Majesty.

QUEEN VIC. This is it?

AIDE. Yes, Ma'am.

> *She considers the painting.*

QUEEN VIC. They look fucked.

AIDE. They do, Ma'am.

QUEEN VIC. I like it. I will buy it.

AIDE. Ma'am.

The AIDE *begins to leave.*

QUEEN VIC. Who is the artist?

AIDE. A Miss Thompson, Ma'am.

QUEEN VIC. A woman?

AIDE. Yes, Ma'am.

QUEEN VIC. How fabulous.

AIDE. Quite.

QUEEN VIC. I want to send Miss Thompson a gift. A bracelet. Nothing too ostentatious. Pearls.

AIDE. Yes, Ma'am.

QUEEN VIC. And an emerald. A large one. The girl deserves it.

The AIDE *exits.*

Miss Thompson. They will be shitting themselves.

NINE – 'MY LOVE IS POLITICAL. MY BODY IS POLITICAL. I TALK EVEN WHEN I DON'T SPEAK'

CORA, FRANCES *and* MARY *are surrounding* ELIZABETH, *who is loving the attention, they all eat cake.* ALICE *rushes in, she is a little out of breath.*

ALICE. Elizabeth?

ELIZABETH. Do not shout. We are right here. Girls, my little sister, Alice.

MARY. Mary. Frances. And / Cora.

ELIZABETH. Or as you will have heard me refer to them, Big Grenadier, Double Eyeglass and Fruit Bowl.

ALICE. It is a pleasure to finally put faces, and names, to Elizabeth's basic descriptions.

ELIZABETH. They do not mind.

FRANCES. Well…

ELIZABETH. It is said with affection.

MARY. Cake?

ALICE. Yes, thank you.

ELIZABETH (*to* ALICE). You look flustered, where have you been?

ALICE. The academy.

FRANCES. Oh, you are an artist too?

ALICE. A poet.

MARY. Ah. Capital.

ELIZABETH. And an activist.

FRANCES. Really?

ALICE. Yes. (*Slight pause.*) To simply exist, as me, is activism.

ELIZABETH. She's extremely good at it. You're very into suffrage at the moment, aren't you, Alice?

ALICE. It is not a whim.

ELIZABETH. I did not say it was.

MARY. Sounds like a fine venture.

ALICE. It is all linked. Courage calls to courage.

CORA. I'm not sure I have the constitution for activism. It's very shouty, is it not? You must be very brave.

ALICE. Not particularly.

ELIZABETH. She cries a lot.

ALICE. I get frustrated.

ELIZABETH. It is a poet thing.

FRANCES. Sounds like you have a real passion for it. We should talk, I am currently quite involved myself.

ALICE. Really?

ALICE *and* FRANCES *talk together, they are excited.* ELIZABETH *is obviously bored and forces* MARY *and* CORA *to pay her some attention. The conversation between* ALICE *and* FRANCES *is the important one, this is the one we should tune into, although* ELIZABETH *obviously disagrees.*

FRANCES. Do you know of Sarah Parker Remond? I heard her lecture the other week, and she was such an inspiration. She warns of the movement becoming exclusionary, as it is in America. We are in danger of it I fear.

ELIZABETH. Do you know, I might go to the academy myself later. It is frightfully good fun. I do not think I could ever become bored of the attention.

ALICE. There are plenty of us that want to stand together though. We must simply ensure that we have the loudest voices.

CORA. I've been a fair amount. Such fun. Not that I get nearly as much attention as you, Elizabeth, obviously but it is nice to be recognised / occasionally...

ELIZABETH. Isn't that quite obvious? Shouting.

ALICE. I didn't mean it literally.

MARY. Although sometimes having a jolly good shout works wonders too.

FRANCES. We could do with your lungs, Mary.

MARY. Oh, I'm not an activist.

ALICE. Never say never.

CORA. I think it would be never for me, I'm much better at having a quiet / little chit-chat.

ELIZABETH (*bored that the conversation has been away from her for so long*). So why were you at the academy?

ALICE. Mamma wanted to go, again.

ELIZABETH. And...was it marvellous?

ALICE. Well, it was quite overwhelming actually.

ELIZABETH. What do you mean?

ALICE. I think you were right.

ELIZABETH. I usually am.

ALICE. People are calling for your election. It is all they are talking about. When the crowd discovered that we were your family, Mamma announced it –

ELIZABETH. Of course.   FRANCES. Subtle.

ALICE. – we were completely surrounded. People shaking our hands, congratulating us. Telling us that you will be an RA within the year. Mamma was pressed into telling them everything about you, they were beside themselves. In the end I had to leave her there.

CORA. Gosh, will she be alright?

ALICE. Oh yes, she can talk about Elizabeth for hours. It is her favourite subject.

ELIZABETH. It really is.

MARY. Splendid.

ALICE. I had to come home. I had to tell you.

MARY. This is simply,   CORA. Wow, Elizabeth.
goodness, how marvellous.

ELIZABETH. Yes, things really are moving. I mean, I knew they would but still, it feels almost inevitable now.

FRANCES. Absolutely.

ALICE. Yes, which is why I think with a little pressure / you could…

ELIZABETH. Oh. No.

CORA. Pressure?

ALICE. You could really change things, politically.

ELIZABETH. Alice.

ALICE. This is greater than you, Elizabeth.

ELIZABETH. No.

ALICE. Yes.

ELIZABETH. I will not throw away what I have achieved by trying to be revolutionary.

ALICE. You must see the bigger picture.

MARY. Which is what?

ALICE. That Elizabeth's success could be the start of something. It could be the spark. It could benefit all of us. Elizabeth has shown that they are open to change.

FRANCES. They will need persuading surely, a little push in the right direction perhaps?

CORA. What do you mean by 'push'? It sounds a little brash.

ALICE. Elizabeth has a platform now.

FRANCES. Influence?

ALICE. Yes, she can use her voice. They will listen to her.

ELIZABETH. And jeopardise all that I have gained.

ALICE. No.

ELIZABETH. But that is what will happen.

ALICE. I don't think so.

ELIZABETH. What Alice doesn't understand is that it's a fine balance. Yes, I have achieved a great deal but it is only the beginning for me. I have so much further to go.

ALICE. I agree. And I will support you in that, of course. But you have to understand that the further you go, Elizabeth, the further we all go.

ELIZABETH. Why must I have the success of all of you on my shoulders?

ALICE. Do you not want others to succeed?

ELIZABETH. I don't know.

Beat as they all look at her.

Fine, yes, if they deserve it.

ALICE. Like you deserved it?

ELIZABETH. I did deserve it. I do deserve it.

ALICE. And your friends, for example, they have talent too? So they deserve it. They should be allowed to succeed as well.

MARY. I'm not sure how comfortable we all are with this actually.

FRANCES. Speak for yourself.

ALICE. It is important for her to understand.

CORA. Absolutely. Understand what?

ALICE. They deserve it, do they not?

ELIZABETH. You are embarrassing me in front of my friends.

ALICE. I simply do not understand why you won't try and help them.

ELIZABETH. Stop.

ALICE. I understand that all women is unimaginable but these three women. You could help them. You could champion their work. Demand that they get considered too. It would be a start. Why won't you do that?

ELIZABETH. You are oversimplifying everything.

ALICE. I just want to understand, Mimi.

ELIZABETH. Because why should I? Why should I have to share this? It's my success. Mine. No one else's. I worked hard to get here. I was clever. I didn't just paint the usual fruit and flowers like the rest of them. /

CORA. What is wrong with fruit and flowers?

FRANCES. Nothing.

ELIZABETH. I adapted my style, I made myself stand out. I discovered the secret to getting noticed, why would I ever want to share that with anyone? Why should I have to?

Pause.

CORA. This really is delicious cake.

MARY. Quite.

ELIZABETH. If I were a man you wouldn't be saying this. You would let me be successful for me alone.

ALICE. But you aren't a man.

ELIZABETH. No. More's the pity.

ELIZABETH *and* ALICE *exit, leaving the friends standing awkwardly.*

TEN – PANIC! THE WOMEN ARE COMING

MILLAIS. There is much talk of her election.

RA THREE. Her what?   RA TWO. Fuck off.

MILLAIS. Her nomination, into the academy.

RA ONE. Are you serious?

MILLAIS. Of course. Were we not expecting this?

RA ONE (*beat*). Yes. Of course.

RA THREE. Wait, so the public want her to become a Royal Academician? / That's impossible.

MILLAIS. Yes. The public, artists, critics. She's very popular.

RA TWO. But she's a woman.

MILLAIS. Exactly, I think that adds to her appeal.

RA ONE. I think that is her appeal. But, yes, of course. The academy is open to everyone.

RA THREE. Everyone.

MILLAIS. This could be a really great thing for us too.

RA THREE. Oh, so great.

RA TWO. Women?

MILLAIS. It is not like we have never had women within our walls. Two of our founding members were women after all.

RA TWO. Exactly. Is that not enough?

MILLAIS. That was over a hundred years ago.

RA TWO. Your point is?

RA THREE. We must reside ourselves to this becoming our norm then?

RA TWO. Damn.

RA ONE. Although...

RA TWO. Yes?

RA ONE. Should they not be satisfied now?

MILLAIS How do you mean?

RA ONE. Well, she has proven that there is no barrier for women. Not at the academy. Women can get their art into the best positions. It is all quite fair.

RA TWO. I quite agree.

RA ONE. Surely now that these barriers are gone, and we have proved ourselves to be a fair and liberal institution, the press will finally stop harking on about elitism, and favouritism, and nepotism.

RA THREE. Quite right, Uncle. It is so boring.

MILLAIS. I do not think that Miss Thompson will go away that quietly, and we should not want her to. Come on, this is extraordinary. And I am not the only one that thinks so, the public are clearly on board. And the press, believe it or not. We are more popular than we've been in years because of her, and now they are waiting to see how far we dare go. So, what do we dare do? How brave are we? I for one want to lead the way. I want history to see that it was this 'Liberal Institution' that started it all. We could elect a woman. Think about it. Think what that would mean. Oh my goodness it is so galvanising.

RA ONE. Yes, galvanising. These are galvanising times. I hope she is enjoying her moment in history. But I cannot help wondering if it is just that. A moment. A blip. She is new and fresh and I worry that she will be in favour for the year and then she will disappear. Along with these calls for her election. And then where would we be? Stuck with a woman RA that has painted one good picture. I mean, of course, absolutely, her election should be considered if she continues to create masterpieces. But off of one painting?

RA THREE. No. And you know, it is probably a lucky fluke. It would be highly embarrassing for her, if we let her in, only for her to create dud after dud.

RA ONE. Precisely. I do not want to put such pressure on the young lady. It would not be fair. No, best we ignore these frankly silly calls for her election. It will go away. She will go away.

MILLAIS. And if she does not?

RA TWO. Then she is a fool.

RA ONE. I will say something to her.

MILLAIS. What?

RA ONE. Nothing much, just some fatherly advice.

ELEVEN – BESSIE AT THE EXHIBITION

BESSIE *is at the Summer Exhibition. They walk into Gallery Two. It's completely packed with people. Everyone is bigger than them. They are pushed and squeezed.*

BESSIE. I'm here. I'm at the Summer Exhibition. Me. It took me longer to get my shilling together than I thought, but I'm here, at last. I've borrowed my sister's dress and it's feeling really good, sort of special. I need to get it back before she notices, but right now I don't really care. I'm fabulous.

They look around.

Blimey, there are a lot people here, and a lot of art. I've been thinking about you and your painting so much that I sort of forgot there'd be other paintings too. But they're everywhere. I sketched a picture of a dead dog yesterday, it was in the alley outside the factory, all sad eyed and stiff. I really liked it, my picture, but seeing all these, I dunno, how are you ever meant to stand out? This should be an aspiring artist's dream, but I'm starting to feel a bit sick, it feels, it feels a lot. Because this is probably the most important moment of my life so far. Why is everyone so big? So tall. So posh. Stop shaking, Bess. Just duck, under, here, and. There. Whoa.

They stare at The Roll Call, *taking it all in.*

TWELVE – A LITTLE WORD OF ADVICE

At the academy. ELIZABETH *is admiring the crowd surrounding* Roll Call. BESSIE *is still staring.* RA ONE *enters and watches* ELIZABETH *for a while. He slithers towards her, making her jump slightly as he talks into her ear.*

RA ONE. One of the RAs have requested a rail.

ELIZABETH. Sorry?

RA ONE. A rail. To be installed along the whole of that wall. To protect his painting from your adoring public.

ELIZABETH. I do not think they are my adoring public.

RA ONE. Don't be modest. Of course they are.

He watches her.

His request was denied.

ELIZABETH. I am sure no one would damage his painting.

RA ONE. Not intentionally.

ELIZABETH. Is that not why the policeman has been stationed where he has?

RA ONE. He is there for the protection of your painting, Miss Thompson. To stop the surge of your gaping admirers. Our poor RA has no such protection. But do not fret your young, lovely head about it. His is a far less accomplished work, it doesn't deserve protection. Now tell me, how are you enjoying all of this popularity?

ELIZABETH. It's unfathomable.

RA ONE. There you go again with that modesty. Tell me what you truly think.

ELIZABETH. Well, it's flattering.

RA ONE. You enjoy watching the droves struggle and squeeze as they try and get a good look?

ELIZABETH. I'm not sure I…

RA ONE. I'm teasing.

ELIZABETH. Oh.

RA ONE. It's a tad revolting really, is it not? The public can be so grotesque in their admirations. Their raptures can seem quite unmeaning and ignorant. It can all feel quite cheap. I'm not saying that the painting or yourself is cheap, gosh no, simply the general public.

ELIZABETH. It's touched a lot of people.

RA ONE. Yes. So I hear. Tears flowing out of them like little babies. Little baby girls.

ELIZABETH. The public want to see the physical and psychological effects of war on the anonymous soldier. It is a moving subject. They are tired of the usual plunging horses.

RA ONE. Quite.

ELIZABETH. I do not paint for the glory of war, I think my adoring public appreciate that.

RA ONE. How insightful.

Pause.

Can I give you a word of advice, Miss Thompson?

ELIZABETH. Of course.

RA ONE. Beware the dangers of sudden popularity. It may feel like you are unstoppable now, with the public on your side. The world is your oyster. It is yours for the taking. And so forth. And yet, some would call your success a 'lucky fluke'.

ELIZABETH. Would they?

RA ONE. Yes. It is easy to produce one successful work, to produce multiple would be… um, wait… oh, what is the word?

ELIZABETH. Extraordinary?

RA ONE. Foolish. I don't want you to feel disappointed when life returns to normal for you.

ELIZABETH. Maybe it won't.

RA ONE. And yet, I feel that it will. Well, perhaps this is one of those things where we can not see eye to eye. We are very different after all. I an artist, you a woman.

ELIZABETH. Yes. Perhaps.

> ELIZABETH *and* RA ONE *stay in Gallery Two, 'admiring' the other art, as the next scene takes place.*

THIRTEEN – BESSIE IN LOVE

BESSIE *hasn't moved.*

BESSIE. Oh, Elizabeth. He is dead. Definitely. His skin is a kind of greyie-green. Dead colour. It's so beautiful.

They sense someone standing next to them but don't look around.

This well-to-do gent has just slotted in beside me. I'm gonna sneak a look at him, 'cause I'm a nosy scamp. Oh, he's crying. Miss Thompson, Elizabeth, he's crying. Fat tears are silently dripping from his eyeballs onto these beautiful polished floorboards. Splish, splash, splosh. Y'know, I'm right tempted to pat him on the head, but do you think he'll take offense if I touch him? I don't fancy explaining a reddened cheek to Ma, 'specially as she doesn't know I'm here. Or that I'm in this dress. But I want him to know that I understand. That's what you do. You make us feel. You make us remember all the pain we've ever felt. Through art. That's why I love you. Sorry. Can I say that? I mean, I do love you. And I know that you'll probably never know that. But that doesn't make it less real, right? (*Beat.*) I should tell someone.

I should tell this gent. I think he'll understand, because I think he probably loves you too, and weirdly I'm okay with that. Because we're feeling it together. Loving you together. Two people who couldn't be more different, this gentleman and me. So, I reach out my sneaky-cheeky fingers and tug his sleeve. One gentle tug. Y'know, just to say, 'I feel you, Sir. I love her too.' And one day, one day, Elizabeth, you might even love me back.

Song: 'Crushing'

BESSIE.

> *I can be your best friend*
> *If you want*
> *Your favourite, mostly best friend*
> *If you want*
> *You can paint me*
> *And I'll plait your hair*
> *Tell me secrets*
> *Wear your underwear*
>
> *'Cause I've got a*
> *Crush*
> *You know I got one,*
> *Oo-oo just an innocent*
> *Crush*
> *There's no harm done 'cause I only want to*
> *Love you, hold you, be you*
> *Make you my best friend because your talent makes me*
> *Feel all weird inside*
>
> *Uh, uh, a fizzy little bomb of love*
> *I should be your sweet one*
> *If you want*
> *Your favourite, sparkly sweet one*
> *If you want*
> *We'll be inseparable*
> *You and me*
> *Touching skin*
> *And feel electricity*

> *More than a*
> *Crush*
> *You're my goddess*
> *Oo-oo it's a serious*
> *Crush*
> *Now notice me 'cause I only want to*
> *Love you, hold you, be you*
> *Make you my best friend because your talent makes me*
> *Feel all weird inside*
> *Uh, uh, a fizzy little bomb of love.*

RA ONE *passes by* BESSIE. BESSIE *can't hold in their excitement and turns to him, having no idea who he is or that* ELIZABETH *is tantalisingly near.*

Excuse me, sir? This artist, she is going to change everything, for all of us.

BESSIE *leaves, oblivious that they are oh so close to* ELIZABETH.

RA ONE (*seeking out* ELIZABETH). Just promise me that you will enjoy this time. While it lasts.

ELIZABETH. Absolutely. Great advice.

RA ONE *exits*.

FOURTEEN – 'PRESSURE IS A PRIVILEGE – IT ONLY COMES TO THOSE WHO EARN IT'

ELIZABETH *is alone. She takes out her paintbrush and begins to paint* Quatre Bras, *her next masterpiece.*

ELIZABETH (*to herself*). Do not fail.

FIFTEEN – 'HAVE A BIG CRAZY DREAM AND SEE WHERE IT TAKES YOU'

ELIZABETH *continues painting* Quatre Bras. ALICE *and* FRANCES *enter.* ELIZABETH *hardly notices their existence.*

FRANCES. Has she moved?

ALICE. Not in days.

FRANCES. I wish I had an ounce of her determination, I would get so much shit sorted.

ALICE. You are doing fine, Frances.

FRANCES. I could do better.

ALICE. We are quite a single-minded family when we need to be.

FRANCES. It shows. A successful artist, and now a published poet as well. Your mamma must be fit to burst.

ALICE. My mamma has the charming quality of being a bottomless pit when it comes to pride.

FRANCES. Sounds nice.

ALICE. Are you busy?

FRANCES. I find that my art doesn't feel as important at the moment.

ALICE. Have you ever thought about painting for the movement?

FRANCES. What do you mean?

ALICE. Paint about suffrage, document it.

FRANCES. I am not sure that my version of suffrage would sell.

ALICE. It might.

FRANCES. Only certain women would be able to buy it. I am not sure they would want what I paint.

ALICE. Could you compromise?

FRANCES. Should I have to?

ALICE. No, sorry. I just think that art could play a large role in persuading people. It would be an excellent use of your talents. You could paint what is happening, or, or what we want to happen. Yes, and then we could distribute copies, or pay for an advertisement in the paper, really get the word, no, really get the picture, out there.

FRANCES. I need to sell my work.

ALICE. Yes, I know, but this needn't take up too much of your time, and I think it would sell, after a while. Just think of all those people opening up their newspapers on a Monday morning and being faced with what the movement really is.

FRANCES. I would not paint what people want to see.

ALICE. You would not need to, it is not about placating them. Come on, Frances, you complain about not doing enough, well this would put you right in the centre of everything. That's the dream, is it not?

FRANCES. This utopian movement you are imagining is exciting, of course it is. I would love to paint real Black women, working, mothering, fighting for what we deserve. But I think you are being naive, no newspaper would print them. I would not do it for free, and I cannot imagine anyone paying me to do it. I think the majority of suffragists wouldn't want to see my pictures either. I love your idealism, Alice, but it is a luxury I cannot afford.

ALICE. I'm sorry. I wasn't thinking.

FRANCES. Perhaps you should find someone else to paint these pictures?

ALICE. Yes. Perhaps.

ELIZABETH. Before you ask, I'm not doing it.

SIXTEEN – ONE YEAR LATER AND SHE COMES. AGAIN. SELFISH COW (FYI IT'S 1875)

A year has passed, it is 1875. The RAS *and* MILLAIS *saunter on.*

RA ONE. Another year, another haul of exhibition hopefuls.

RA TWO. And Miss Thompson? Has she sent?

RA ONE. I do not know.

RA THREE. The rumour is yes.

RA TWO. Fabulous.

RA THREE. Quite.

RA ONE. She does not listen to friendly advice, apparently.

MILLAIS. I do not wish to appear smug but I did say this would happen.

RA TWO. And is it… good?

RA THREE. Oh yes. Superior even.

RA TWO. Superior?

RA THREE. Greatly. That is the rumour. Spread mostly by herself.

RA TWO. So it might be terrible?

MILLAIS. You are scared.

RA TWO. I am a man.

MILLAIS. You are all terrified that it will be a masterpiece and we will have to stop ignoring the calls for her election and actually do something about it.

RA ONE. Having a woman elected will not be the rosy, liberal dream that you naively imagine it to be. We did a great thing last year. Hanging her painting in the most favourable of positions. We did that. This liberal institution.

MILLAIS. And that is close enough?

RA ONE. Yes. In my opinion.

RA TWO. I agree.

MILLAIS (*to* RA THREE). And you? Do you have an opinion of your own?

RA THREE. Yes, yes I do. Actually. It would be a big change, having a woman in. I'm not too good with change.

RA ONE. I suggest you drop it. She is not to be one of us.

MILLAIS. And if the rumours are true?

RA ONE. And she has painted a masterpiece?

    MILLAIS *gives the slightest of nods.*

    Then we will exhibit it. Of course.

RA TWO. Bollocks.

RA ONE. But I am not having her become the fake shining star that she was last year. Working the public up into a frenzy. That is where all this election nonsense came from in the first place. Weak-minded people getting caught up in her celebrity. It's cheap. I will not have the academy cheapened.

MILLAIS. You are ridiculous. Her popularity is a good thing for us. We should be hanging her work in Gallery Two again, we should be celebrating her.

RA ONE. No. We will accept her, we will hang her, but that is it.

RA THREE. Quite right, all this fame nonsense needs to be put to bed.

MILLAIS. So what? You want to sky her? Put her in Gallery Eight? You are fools if you think that will stop the public adoring her. Wherever we hang her painting she will be a star once more. And rightly so.

RA ONE. Yes, if they see her painting.

MILLAIS. What?

RA ONE. I agree, if they see her painting then she will be a star. Therefore is it not fortuitous that we have a room where stars are sent to die?

MILLAIS. No. You cannot be serious.

RA ONE. Deadly.

SEVENTEEN – A STAR IS DYING

ELIZABETH, ALICE, CORA, FRANCES *and* MARY *look out at the audience, they are admiring* ELIZABETH's *latest painting,* Quatre Bras.

CORA. More soldiers.

MARY. What is it called?

ELIZABETH. *The 28th Regiment at Quatre Bras.*

FRANCES. Snappy.

CORA. Why does that one look so strange?

ELIZABETH. Which one?

CORA. That one. He's all pale.

ELIZABETH. He's been shot in the stomach. The pain is excruciating. His blood and guts are oozing from his punctured torso. He'll be dead within minutes.

MARY. Splendid.

ELIZABETH. Do you like it?

FRANCES. It's magnificent.

ELIZABETH. It is, isn't it?

FRANCES. Yes. As I said.

CORA. I think it's better than *Roll Call* even.

MARY. Absolutely.

CORA. I wonder where will they hang it? If it is better than *Roll Call*, which it is, absolutely, then it deserves a better position. But there is no better position than Gallery Two, on the line, is there? Gosh, it is a conundrum.

MARY. Quite.

ALICE. Maybe the RAs will discover a whole new location within the academy walls for this masterpiece? The front door perhaps?

CORA. Oh, yes. What a wonderful thought.

ELIZABETH. She is being facetious.

CORA. Oh. Do you not like it?

ELIZABETH. She is vexed by my attitude. I am being arrogant again.

FRANCES. You own it well.

ELIZABETH. Precisely. I think that annoys her all the more.

ALICE. Don't speak for me, Mimi.

ELIZABETH. But that is right, is it not?

ALICE. No.

MARY. Have you had any word from the academy?

ELIZABETH. Not yet. But as the darling of last years' exhibition I'm expecting some serious fawning.

ALICE. And what about the 'advice'?

FRANCES. What is this?

ELIZABETH. Oh nothing.

ALICE. She was warned off.

MARY. Really?

ELIZABETH. No. It was nothing. I am still their sweetheart. Only last week one of them, I forget which one, told me that the academy had never received so many daily shillings before, and that it ought to present me with a diamond necklace. I know. They love me. I must tell them that I am still waiting.

There is a knock on the door. MARY *looks out the window.*

MARY. It is that man from the Hanging Committee.

FRANCES. Oh, I cannot stand him. Excuse me while I hide.

FRANCES *exits and performs a miraculous transformation to become* HANGING COMMITTEE. *He enters.*

HANGING COMMITTEE. Miss Thompson?

ELIZABETH.Yes.

HANGING COMMITTEE. Miss Elizabeth Thompson?

ELIZABETH. Yes. Yes. I am her. We have met, many times. Please do not go into all of that again. He is a stickler for clarification this one.

HANGING COMMITTEE. Best to be sure.

MARY. Quite.

ALICE. You have news?

HANGING COMMITTEE. Yes. Miss Thompson, your painting has been accepted.

CORA. That's marvellous.

ELIZABETH. Where?

HANGING COMMITTEE. Oh, um, let me just see.

He looks in his notes.

ELIZABETH. Well?

MARY. Gallery Two. Must be.

HANGING COMMITTEE. No.

ELIZABETH. No?

HANGING COMMITTEE. No, let me just… yes, here we are.

ELIZABETH. And?

HANGING COMMITTEE. The lecture room.

MARY. Where?

HANGING COMMITTEE. The lecture room.

ELIZABETH. Where the fuck / is the lecture room?

ALICE. Elizabeth. Don't.

HANGING COMMITEE. In Burlington House.

ELIZABETH. No it isn't.

HANGING COMMITEE. Ah yes. Yes it is.

ELIZABETH. I have never heard of it.

HANGING COMMITTEE. Ladies, I must depart. Very busy.

CORA. Elizabeth?   ELIZABETH. Why will you
                                    not tell me where it is?

HANGING COMMITTEE. I did. The lecture room.

ELIZABETH. For fuck /…

ALICE. Yes, but where is   CORA. Elizabeth?
    that?

HANGING COMMITEE. In Burlington / House.

MARY. Don't be ridiculous   ELIZABETH. You really are a
    man.   little / [shit]

HANGING COMMITTEE. I
    must take my leave. Lots of artists to deliver good news to.
    I can't be chit-chatting to you ladies all day. Farewell. Gosh,
    so pretty.

He takes his leave.

MARY. This is absurd.

ELIZABETH. What does it mean that none of us have heard of
    it?

ALICE. Nothing.   CORA. Elizabeth.

MARY. Perhaps it's a fabulous new gallery. We did say that
  your painting would need somewhere special.

CORA. Elizabeth.   ELIZABETH. This doesn't
                                   make any sense.

CORA.Elizabeth, will you listen to me?

  They all look at CORA.

  I know the lecture room.

ELIZABETH. What?

MARY. Do you?

CORA. I exhibited last year and / it was positioned there.

MARY. Did you?

CORA. Yes.

ALICE. I did not know you had exhibited too.

MARY. None of us did. Why keep it so quiet?

CORA. It did not seem such a great thing in the wake of
  Elizabeth's resounding success.

ALICE. Of course it was great.

MARY. Being part of the Summer Exhibition, wherever you are
  hung, is a wonderful triumph. I only wish we had known.
  I would have thought I would have recognised your work
  though, how did I not see it?

CORA. You may not have been to the lecture room.

MARY. I'm fairly sure I went to all the galleries.

CORA. Well, possibly not. The lecture room, it... you can go
  round and around the galleries in a loop and never find your
  way into it.

ELIZABETH. The black hole.

ALICE. What?

CORA. Yes. I'm sorry.

ELIZABETH. The lecture room is the black hole. I've been black-holed.

ALICE. I'm sorry, I have absolutely no idea what...

CORA. The black hole is the lecture room's more common name. The only dark room in the whole place. The light is almost blue compared to the golden sun-glow in the others.

MARY. It's where paintings go to be, well, where they...

ELIZABETH. Go to be forgotten. I've been forgotten.

ALICE. No, Mimi, you haven't.

ELIZABETH. They do not like it. It is not good enough.

MARY. It is a brilliant work.

ELIZABETH. Do not lie to me. Only inferior artists are black-holed.

MARY (*to* CORA). She does not mean that.

ELIZABETH. Yes I do.

ALICE. But you have still been accepted, they could have turned your work away but they did not. That is positive.

ELIZABETH. Do not speak about things that you do not understand, Alice. I would rather have been rejected, this, this black hole is an insult. They are granting me a favour, popping my painting somewhere where it won't offend. Bless her, she tried, she failed. It's a piece of shit. Clearly.

ALICE. Mimi...

ELIZABETH. Leave me alone. All of you.

They linger.

Just fuck off.

ELIZABETH *is left alone. We see her crumple, all her sparkle dies.*

EIGHTEEN – 'THE TRUTH WILL SET YOU FREE, BUT FIRST IT WILL PISS YOU OFF'

BESSIE *is wandering around Burlington House looking for the lecture room.*

BESSIE. It has to be here somewhere. (*They read from the leaflet.*) 'Miss Elizabeth Thompson. The *28th Regiment at Quatre Bras*. The lecture room.'

  ELIZABETH *enters the lecture room. She stares at her painting.* MILLAIS *enters.*

MILLAIS. Ah, Miss Thompson, good morning.

ELIZABETH. You were a part of the decision, were you not?

MILLAIS. It is complicated.

ELIZABETH. You black-holed me.

MILLAIS. They hung you in the lecture room. On the line, in the lecture room. Really quite a prime location within the room…

ELIZABETH. Don't.

MILLAIS. The eye really is drawn directly to your painting as you enter.

ELIZABETH. If you enter.

  No one who matters will see it. (*Beat.*) Is it really that inferior?

MILLAIS What?

ELIZABETH. My painting?

MILLAIS. No. No.

ELIZABETH. I believed it to be a mountain compared to the hill of *The Roll Call*. Am I deluded? I look at it and I see mastery, pure skill. Have I become so blinded by success that I can not see when I produce a complete failure?

MILLAIS. I think it came from a place of necessity.

ELIZABETH. Of course.

MILLAIS. Protection of… protecting all the work. All the…

ELIZABETH. Artists.

>RA ONE *and* RA THREE *enter with* ALICE *in tow,*
>MILLAIS *and* ELIZABETH *don't notice.*

MILLAIS.…Look it is still a great achievement. One that most women would appreciate as the accomplishment that it is.

ELIZABETH. Oh, I am more than an accomplished woman, sir. I am an artist. Like you.

>A professional artist.

MILLAIS. Please, Miss Thompson, calm down.

ELIZABETH. Why? Are you frightened that I might get angry?

>ALICE *rushes up to* ELIZABETH.

ALICE (*just for* ELIZABETH). Women that are angry are a dangerous thing.

ELIZABETH. Alice. Look at it.

ALICE. I know, but not like this.

RA THREE. We must admit that we were all quite doubtful that you would be able to send in any important picture this year.

RA ONE. What with the load and responsibility of your almost overwhelming success last year.

RA THREE. But you have. And such a difficult one.

>It really was very plucky of you.

ELIZABETH. And yet, here it is.

RA ONE. Indeed. Here it is.

RA THREE. Hanging within Burlington House.

RA ONE. At our Summer Exhibition.

>*Pause.*

ALICE. Mimi?

ELIZABETH. What?

ALICE. Mamma has organised a champagne lunch.

We should hurry.

RA ONE. Yes. Hurry. Go enjoy yourself. Mimi.

*ALICE drags ELIZABETH away, trying to calm her
spiralling panic.*

Song: 'Black-Holed'

ELIZABETH.
> *Spiralling, spiralling*
> *Out of control*
> *This does not happen to me*
> *Spiralling, spiralling*
> *I can't grab hold*
> *Screaming, falling, lost at sea*

*BESSIE enters the lecture room, unsure of where they are.
They carry a leaflet with them.*

BESSIE. Wait. Is this it?

*BESSIE realises that the lecture room is the black hole. They
see the painting but do not notice ELIZABETH who is being
propped up by ALICE.*

Song: 'Black-Holed'

BESSIE.
> *She's been black-holed*
> *Hate it, hate them too*
> *It's a supermassive crime alright*
> *To black-hole her*
> *How dare they do that?*
> *How dare they do that?*
> *Her fans are gonna kick, scream, bite, fight*

NINETEEN – BUBBLES, HIDE MY SHAME

ELIZABETH *and* ALICE *are drinking champagne. They are both drunk. They are both angry.*

ELIZABETH. I need more drink.

ALICE. There isn't any /

ELIZABETH. How dare they?

ALICE. You've drunk it all.

ELIZABETH. Acting like I should be grateful.

ALICE. It's despicable.

ELIZABETH. Like I owe them something.

ALICE. I am not even tipsy.

ELIZABETH. They owe me. A diamond necklace my arse.

ALICE. You've been put in your place, young lady.

ELIZABETH. Why? I do not understand it.

ALICE *picks up the empty champagne bottles.*

ALICE. Empty.

ELIZABETH. I've been playing by their rules the whole fucking time.

ALICE. Mamma will never order enough champagne.

ELIZABETH. Alice?

ALICE. What?

ELIZABETH. Me.

ALICE. Sorry?

ELIZABETH. Why has this happened?

ALICE. You drink too much.

ELIZABETH. The black hole, Alice. Why have they done this to me? It is not fair. Fuck, it makes no sense. They love me.

The men, the RAs, they all adore me. Worship the bloody ground I walk on. I don't understand.

ALICE. I don't know. You scare them, I suppose.

ELIZABETH. Ridiculous, I have no such power over men.

ALICE. Yes you do. Of course you do. You have everything. Just like always.

ELIZABETH. What are you talking about?

ALICE. You inspire people.

ELIZABETH. People? Oh God, no.

ALICE. Perhaps we could send for more?

ELIZABETH. I do not encourage this.

ALICE. Well, do not drink it then.

ELIZABETH. What? Focus. Me.

ALICE. Right. / Of course. Absolutely. You.

ELIZABETH. I have not encouraged people. I do not encourage anyone. I am not calling for revolt amongst the weak and downtrodden.

ALICE. I know.

ELIZABETH. But these are the people they think I inspire?

ALICE. The weak and downtrodden?

ELIZABETH *reluctantly nods*.

Not the words I would choose, but yes.

ELIZABETH. But I have not said anything. I am only interested in me. I have not asked for them to open their doors to anyone else and yet they punish me. It's not fair, why would they do that?

ALICE. Because you are a bloody beacon of hope.

ELIZABETH. Fuck.

ALICE. You don't even have to say anything and people love you. It's like you're the bloody bringer of change. It's so unfair.

ELIZABETH. Why is there no champagne?

ALICE. And the academy could not have that. So they needed to quieten you. Well, not you, obviously since you don't speak, but what you represent.

ELIZABETH. I don't represent anything. I represent me. It's about me. Me. I thought that was obvious. Do I need to tell them that? Yes, I should tell them that.

ALICE. Who?

ELIZABETH. The academy.

ALICE. What, now?

ELIZABETH (*practising her speech*). Sirs, there has been a mistake. I am not a figurehead. I am not inspiring. I do not encourage. I am just Miss Thompson. Little, sweet, lovely, Miss Thompson. Demure. Grateful /

ALICE. Toady, / arrogant.

ELIZABETH. Exceptionally brilliant. Miss Thompson.

ALICE. And fuck everyone else.

ELIZABETH. Precisely.

Beat. ELIZABETH *finds a half glass of champagne and goes to drink it.*

ALICE. Share that with me.

ELIZABETH. No. It's mine.

ALICE. I believe it was Mamma's.

ELIZABETH. Well, now it is mine.

ALICE. You really are horribly selfish.

ELIZABETH. You cannot talk to me like that.

ALICE. Why not? It's the truth.

ELIZABETH. Is this about the champagne?

ALICE. It is about you, Elizabeth. As always. You will not accept any responsibility. All you do is cower and fawn. It's disgusting.

ELIZABETH. I hardly fawned today.

ALICE. No. Because you were angry.

ELIZABETH. Exactly.

ALICE. Because you had been wronged.

ELIZABETH. Yes. At last you understand.

ALICE. You are infuriating.

ELIZABETH. Oh, please be quiet. For once.

ALICE. You are despicable.

ELIZABETH. And you are boring.

ALICE. Me? All I do is listen. To you. Going on and on and on about how brilliant you are. How much you deserve everything you are getting. Well, well done, I think, yes, I think you do finally deserve it.

She grabs the half-drunk glass off ELIZABETH *and chucks it down her throat.*

ELIZABETH. You really are very arrogant when you are drunk.

ALICE. And you are arrogant all of the time.

ELIZABETH. I cannot believe that you are talking to me like this. I am your sister.

ALICE. And I am yours, Mimi.

ELIZABETH. It's hardly the same.

ALICE. I cannot, I cannot talk to you.

ELIZABETH. At last she shuts up.

ALICE. You. I can't. You truly are…

ELIZABETH. What? What am I, Alice? Come on. Say it. You cannot hurt me with your pompous, smug words. You have preached at me, and lectured me and told me how to be better. And it is so boring. I am so bored by you. All I ever wanted was to enjoy my success. But no, you couldn't allow that. You just had to make me feel guilty. And now something truly awful has happened to me, I have been treated in the most appalling manner and still you chide me. This is shit for me, Alice, so I do not care about anyone else. What this means for anyone else. Even you. (*Beat.*) That is what you are truly thinking. How this setback for me, my black-fucking-hole, will affect you. Miss Alice Thompson, 'Poet Laureate,' it seems a little less likely now, doesn't it? So do not pretend this is about people. You are just as selfish as me. You want success, you want to be at the very top and you thought you could use me to get there. But no one is going to let you be Poet Laureate. Wake up. You are a woman. A lecturing, sanctimonious, bossy woman and you do not have my talent. So get over yourself and leave me alone. Please. It's all just getting so terribly boring.

ALICE *exits, nearly in tears.* ELIZABETH *stands on her own.*

End of Act One.

ACT TWO

TWENTY – 'I CAN SEE THE QUEEN OF ENGLAND GAZING ON MY SHAPE. MAGNIFICENT, SHE MURMURS, MOVING ON'

QUEEN VIC *is carried on.* AIDE *waits for her to start talking. Finally, she does.*

QUEEN VIC. What does it mean? To be black-holed?

AIDE. I think it...

QUEEN VIC. Shut up. I can guess. It will have some deep, unfathomable symbolism to do with the vulva. These things always do.

AIDE. Ma'am.

QUEEN VIC. I said they would shit themselves.

AIDE. Ma'am.

QUEEN VIC. She was a fool to align herself with the 'women's rights' brigade. Nothing can destroy a woman's reputation faster than they can.

AIDE. Yes, Ma'am.

QUEEN VIC. And now they have punished her.

AIDE. Yes, Ma'am.

QUEEN VIC. She should have concealed her power, downplayed her influence, shown that she was not a threat.

AIDE. Like you, Ma'am?

QUEEN VIC. Precisely. Just like me. And yet they will still use my rule to further their cause. It seems a woman at the top will always excite those that are disposed to excitement. My very being is a statement, and those women will use that.

But what they do not seem to grasp is that we women are not made for governing, and if we are good women, we must dislike these masculine occupations.

AIDE. Again, like you, Ma'am?

QUEEN VIC. Me?

AIDE. Yes. You govern but dislike it, it is a burden best suited to a man?

QUEEN VIC. Oh no. I bloody love it.

TWENTY-ONE – 'GOTTA BLAME IT ON MY JUICE'

ELIZABETH *tentatively approaches* ALICE. *It is the morning after and they are both hungover.*

ELIZABETH. My head aches.

ALICE *pointedly ignores her.*

I probably deserve it.

Still nothing.

Alice? Are you not talking to me?

ALICE. What is it you want me to say?

ELIZABETH. I don't know.

Pause.

Would you like me to apologise? I can. I can say sorry if you want me to.

ALICE. No.

ELIZABETH. I do not think you are boring. I don't know why I said that.

ALICE. Do you not?

ELIZABETH. You are an excellent poet.

ALICE. Just not quite excellent enough to become Poet Laureate?

ELIZABETH. Alice /

ALICE. No.

ELIZABETH. Please do not be angry with me.

ALICE. I am not angry.

ELIZABETH. What then? Frustrated? I can be very frustrating, but then I am your sister and remarkably selfish, so obviously that will frustrate you.

ALICE. Do not tell me how I feel.

ELIZABETH. Talk to me then.

ALICE. What is the point? You do not listen.

ELIZABETH. I will.

ALICE (*pause as she considers* ELIZABETH). I do not feel anything.

ELIZABETH. I do not believe that.

ALICE. It is true. I thought I would be angry at you too. But I am not.

ELIZABETH. Why?

ALICE. Because at long last I realise that I cannot change you. I give up. It is actually quite liberating.

ELIZABETH. You give up?

ALICE. Do not take it personally.

ELIZABETH. Right.

ALICE. There will be other women who will succeed, brilliantly bossy ones who will be willing to help the rest of us. You were right, you are not the person to change things.

ELIZABETH. You do not think I will become an RA?

ALICE. I did not say that.

ELIZABETH. But I thought my mere presence at the academy was inciting change. If I become an RA that will change how things work.

ALICE. Do not pretend to be naive, Elizabeth, it does not suit you. We both know that if you become an RA you will slot into the system, become one of the lads, and that helps no one.

ELIZABETH. So you believe I could still become an RA?

ALICE. You are relentlessly single minded.

ELIZABETH. Sorry.

Pause.

ALICE. Yes, I believe it is still possible. The black hole was a warning but once you reassure them that you are no threat, give them your speech and prove that you are an insignificant woman, perhaps they will let you in.

Pause.

ELIZABETH. And, you would hate me if I did that?

ALICE. I think it would be a waste.

ELIZABETH. What would you do? If you were me.

Pause as ALICE *considers her sister properly.*

ALICE. I would walk away. I would stop sending to the academy altogether. I would ignore them, shun them even. Then I would send my brilliant work elsewhere. I would talk loudly, perhaps even shout, a little, about why I'm not sending to the academy.

ELIZABETH. And that will work?

ALICE. They will not like you talking about them, but eventually I believe they will miss you. Having a woman close makes them look good, they will want you back in the fold. You will then be in a position of power. It is up to you what to do with it.

TWENTY-TWO – THE LADY VANISHES

RA ONE, RA TWO, RA THREE *and* MILLAIS *enter.*

RA TWO. So, she's stepping aside, is she?

RA THREE. Apparently she needs time away from the academy.

RA TWO. Remarkable.

RA ONE. Yes, her arrogance is astounding.

RA THREE. After everything we have done for her.

RA TWO. And she will not send to the exhibition again?

RA THREE. That is what she says. Not until there is change.

RA TWO. Bitch. Trying to make us look like small-minded fools. We are the ones that accepted her bloody painting in the first place. We made her a star. And now…

RA THREE. She is greedily demanding more.

MILLAIS. Do not pretend that you would not do the same.

RA THREE. What?

MILLAIS. We are all ambitious. If we had had the success that Miss Thompson had, I think, I know I would have striven for more. Demanded more.

RA ONE. But you are a man. Are you not?

MILLAIS. Yes.

RA ONE. Precisely.

MILLAIS. That is your / argument?

RA ONE. You know, I feel like this strop could benefit the academy.

RA THREE. Oh yes. I feel it too.

RA TWO. How? She is publicly humiliating us.

RA ONE. She believes she is making some sort of statement for sure. But we can weather that storm. We've done it before. People will forget. However, if she had remained.

Continued to send paintings. Good paintings. Then we would have had to exhibit her.

Increasing her fame. Increasing the demand to make her an RA.

RA TWO. I'm not having a damned woman in.

RA ONE. You might not have had the choice.

RA THREE. But who in their right mind would nominate her?

RA ONE. I can think of some.

RA THREE. Good thing we got rid of her then.

MILLAIS. She is the one walking away.

RA THREE. Yes, but we drove her to it. The black hole? Am I right? Lads / lads, lads...

RA ONE. We hung her painting where it needed to be hung. That is all. It was not political. I sincerely hope you have not been telling people otherwise?

RA THREE. No.

RA ONE. Good. But yes. It appears she has gone. And let it be a lesson to us all. We let our guard down. It must never happen again.

TWENTY-THREE – IT'S BEEN THREE YEARS (FYI IT'S NOW 1878)

Three years has passed.

Song: 'Three Years'

RA ONE.

> *It's been three years and nothing*
> *Thank the friggidy frig for that*
> *She never would've fitted within our walls*

A woman's head is too small for a top hat.
Three years is a long time to wait
Feeling nervous she might make her return
But it's been so long now that I can perhaps relax
Safe in the knowledge that all bridges burn.

RA THREE.

It's been three years and nothing
I'm not entirely sure what's going on
That woman hasn't sent any of her art
I'll ask someone if it's a good thing she's gone
Three years is a long time to wait
Not that I've noticed or mind
I've been busy painting some excellent work
All accepted by the academy you'll find

RA TWO.

It's been three years and nothing
Good riddance, don't come back
Except I miss being seen as a good man
My tough exterior is going to crack.
Three years is a long time to wait
To realise I relished being seen as fair
A liberal kind of chap suited me I think
An excellent fellow, with excellent hair.

MILLAIS.

It's been three years and nothing
And I'm feeling like I might have failed
But perhaps it's not actually my fault
She chose to walk away, that ship has sailed.
Three years is a long time to wait
For a woman that clearly doesn't care
I wanted to change the world for the better
She took that away and that's not fair.

TWENTY-FOUR – ELIZABETH WITHOUT THE ACADEMY

ELIZABETH *stands alone, attempting to paint.*

ELIZABETH. Three years. Fuck. And all you've done is send to a handful of mediocre exhibitions with shit art. Congratulations, Elizabeth, you have destroyed your career. (*Shouting offstage.*) This is all your fault, Alice.

ALICE (*from off*). What?

ELIZABETH. Nothing. (*To herself.*) No. Use it. Paint it. Paint. Fucking paint.

TWENTY-FIVE – BESSIE DISAPPOINTED

BESSIE *is standing in Burlington House at the Summer Exhibition 1878.*

BESSIE. Three years. Where are you?

Song: 'Three Years'

> *It's been three years and nothing*
> *Nothing from you on these walls*
> *You've given up like a loser*
> *You're never goin' to be present in these halls.*
> *Three years is a long time to wait*
> *Your fans desperate for news*
> *Come on, tell me please, are you coming back?*
> *Elizabeth, you are not destined to lose.*

TWENTY-SIX – 'HOPE IS A VERY UNRULY EMOTION'

1878. ELIZABETH *is at home, she finishes reading a letter.*
MILLAIS *enters.*

MILLAIS. Miss Thompson.

ELIZABETH. Lady Butler.

MILLAIS. My apologies. Habit. I meant no offence.

ELIZABETH. None taken.

MILLAIS. How is it being a wife?

ELIZABETH. Exhilarating.

MILLAIS. Am I right in thinking he is military?

ELIZABETH. I prefer 'artist's husband'.

MILLAIS. You have not lost your spirit.

ELIZABETH. Were you imagining that I would have?

MILLAIS. I am not sure.

ELIZABETH. I have gained some, I think.

MILLAIS. Capital.

ELIZABETH. Quite.

> *Long pause in which* MILLAIS *stands awkwardly.*
> ELIZABETH *watches, not willing to help him.*

MILLAIS (*nodding to the letter in her hand*). I apologise for
interrupting your correspondence.

ELIZABETH. They are fan letters.

MILLAIS. Ah, you still get those then?

ELIZABETH. Yes. Many.

MILLAIS. It must take many hours to respond.

ELIZABETH. It would, that is why I decided long ago never
to engage in conversation with my fans. I am busy enough
already.

MILLAIS. Yes of course. (*Beat.*) You must be wondering why I am here.

ELIZABETH. I must be.

MILLAIS. You have not sent to the academy in years.

ELIZABETH. No.

MILLAIS. It is a shame. I was hoping to see more of your paintings there. I think you would have seen your work accepted year after year.

ELIZABETH. In more and more obscure locations.

MILLAIS. I'd hope not.

ELIZABETH. Hope is a fool's game, sir.

MILLAIS. I'm sorry to hear you say that. I want to bring you hope right now, you see.

ELIZABETH. How novel.

MILLAIS. There has been much talk in the academy recently. Your work is missed. You are missed.

ELIZABETH. Me?

MILLAIS. You were always alarmingly engaging.

ELIZABETH. Yet I was still passed over.

MILLAIS. I think you could expect more now.

ELIZABETH. In what way?

MILLAIS. How about associate membership?

ELIZABETH. Associate?

MILLAIS. Yes, well I see you have not lost any of your ambition, despite appearances.

ELIZABETH. I am all humility.

MILLAIS. Good. That is good. It will serve you well. It would be best to preserve a womanly reserve if we are to win over the majority.

ELIZABETH. We?

MILLAIS. I am going to nominate you.

ELIZABETH. Right.

MILLAIS. I've surprised you?

ELIZABETH. Maybe a little.

MILLAIS. I believe in you. I believe that you could win.

ELIZABETH. As an associate.

MILLAIS. Baby steps, Lady Butler.

ELIZABETH. I have been patiently waiting for three years, sir.

MILLAIS. And I am hoping that you will wait a little longer, for full membership.

ELIZABETH. I do not want to be stuck as an associate.

MILLAIS. Once you are in I am positive that your charm will see you achieve full membership.

ELIZABETH. Will you nominate me again?

MILLAIS. Yes, me or I'm sure someone will.

ELIZABETH. That is not good enough. I need you to promise it. Say it.

MILLAIS (*beat*). Lady Butler, I will nominate you for associate and in due course, full membership.

ELIZABETH. Thank you.

MILLAIS. It is my pleasure.

ELIZABETH. After three years, I'd barely dared to hope.

MILLAIS. Well then, let us dare again.

TWENTY-SEVEN – 'I JUST LOVE BOSSY WOMEN'

ELIZABETH *and* ALICE *are at* ELIZABETH's *home*.

ALICE. It could actually happen?

ELIZABETH. Apparently so, yes. I will need to make sure I stand out at the summer exhibition this year, make my presence known so it's obvious that I should be voted in. I was thinking about sending in two paintings. What do you think?

ALICE. I think that sounds wonderful. It's so exciting, you are going to be a bossy woman amongst all those men.

ELIZABETH. That is terrifying.

ALICE. I know. But someone has to be the first. And I for one am glad that it will be you.

ELIZABETH. Thank you for not giving up on me.

ALICE. I can see that you are trying.

ELIZABETH. I feel the weight of it, Alice. The weight of them. All the others.

ALICE. As you should. It is bigger than you, Mimi.

ELIZABETH. Fuck.

ALICE. Think of them less as a weight and more as a human pyramid. With you at the top. Doing a jazzy kick.

ELIZABETH. It is too much.

ALICE. Yes. Yes, of course it is. We ask too much of you. I ask too much of you. But it is necessary. You will become the first woman elected into the academy, and you will set a revolution in motion. And people will love you for it. And you will forever be remembered as the Great Elizabeth Thompson.

ELIZABETH. I know what you are doing.

ALICE. I am being too transparent?

ELIZABETH. Yes.

ALICE. I am excited. It is exciting, Mimi. You are exciting. You are delivering hope. The hope that things can change. That we will be in.

ELIZABETH. That I will be in.

ALICE. Yes, you and then the rest of us.

ELIZABETH. And you will be Poet Laureate.

ALICE. It might not even be that long to wait. Tennyson's turning seventy.

ELIZABETH. Oh great, he'll definitely be dead soon.

Song: 'Bossy Women'

ALICE.

> *There will be bossy women everywhere*
> *Fierce, bossy women, with fabulous hair*
> *Not that our looks will count for one jot*
> *Not when our intellect is this smokin' hot*
>
> *Bossy women in every building*
> *In every room, at every table*
> *Bossing to make sure no one is left behind (again)*
> *We'll be there, ready and willing and oh so able*
>
> *'Cause it's our time, girl*
> *It's our time*
> *Bossy women unite*
> *Bossy women it's time to fight*

ELIZABETH. That does sound good.

ALICE.

> *There will be bossy women with the vote*
> *And we'll accept it with grace, we won't gloat*
> *For then we'll be the heads of huge industries*
> *And, fuck it, we'll probably be leading countries*

ELIZABETH. Fuck, is that it?

ALICE. No.

> *We will be politicians.*

ELIZABETH.

> *We'll be experts.*

ALICE.

> *Philosophers.*

ELIZABETH.

> *And superstars.*

ALICE.

> *Our opinions will matter, you'll see*

ELIZABETH.

> *They'll listen, and it'll all down to me*

ALICE.

> *They will welcome us, and share out their power*

ELIZABETH.

> *And nothing will go wrong, it won't turn sour*

ALICE. It won't. Have hope, Mimi.

ELIZABETH.

> *It will all come to pass because of me*
> *Because of wonderful, brilliant me*
> *A human pyramid to hold me up*
> *And me at the top with your winner's cup*
>
> *I'm the woman to show us the way*
> *The one the books will all write about*
> *I'll be the one at the top showing you how it's done*
> *And it'll be my name, Elizabeth, they will shout*

ELIZABETH and ALICE.

> *'Cause it's our time, girl*
> *It's our time*
> *Bossy women unite*
> *Bossy women it's time to fight*

ELIZABETH. No pressure then.

TWENTY-EIGHT – 'THESE ARTISTS TAKE THEMSELVES TOO SERIOUSLY'

QUEEN VIC *appears, she is thoughtful.* AIDE *follows.*

QUEEN VIC. Do you believe that it's possible to feel change?

AIDE. Ma'am?

QUEEN VIC. To feel it approaching, creeping up on us like a little rabid Yorkshire Terrier? Teeth bared, ready to bite.

AIDE. Change could be seen as a good thing. Ma'am.

QUEEN VIC. Perhaps for you. Lowly, insignificant, you. But when you are at the top change is almost exclusively troublesome.

AIDE. Yes, Ma'am.

QUEEN VIC. I liked her, you know, I thought her plucky. And it was fun seeing the men squirm.

AIDE. You do love a squirming man, Ma'am.

QUEEN VIC. I do. But I am disappointed. She's become... encouraging to others.

AIDE. So I hear, Ma'am.

QUEEN VIC. I do not encourage encouragement, it leads to people believing in themselves.

AIDE. I hear she has been particularly encouraging to her sister, Ma'am.

QUEEN VIC. What is this?

AIDE. The poet. There is talk of her being considered for the next Poet Laureate.

QUEEN VIC. Where did you hear this?

AIDE. It is just rumour, Ma'am.

QUEEN VIC. Poet Laureate? Now that would be something. I suppose it is good that that decision is left to me then. I know what to do for the best.

TWENTY-NINE – 'A PLACE YOU CAN LIVE OUT A FANTASY YOU NEVER LIVED BEFORE'

ELIZABETH *is at her parents' house painting two pictures at the same time. It is late and dark.* ALICE *and* MARY *enter, giggling, they don't notice* ELIZABETH, *who continues painting quietly in the shadows.*

ALICE. Thank you for taking me along. It was such fun.

MARY. I thought you would like it. I love to see a woman in a top hat. I find it quite /...

ALICE. Arousing?

MARY. I was going to say stirring.

ALICE. Oh yes, I think she was quite stirred by you too, Mary.

MARY. It is a talent of mine. But you enjoyed it, yes? They are devilishly talented too, are they not? And quite, quite beautiful.

ELIZABETH. Who are?

ALICE. Blimey, Elizabeth. Why are you not at home?

ELIZABETH. Do you know what time it is?

ALICE. Mary took me to the music hall.

ELIZABETH. Does Mamma know?

ALICE. Of course not.

ELIZABETH. Was it safe?

MARY. She was with me.

ELIZABETH. You should not have gone.

MARY. It was a lark.

ELIZABETH. Mary, she is my little sister.

ALICE. It was fine.

ELIZABETH. You risk too much, Alice.

ALICE. Is this about my safety or your reputation?

ELIZABETH. I am not the one getting the reputation.

ALICE. I thought so.

MARY. This was my idea, not Alice's. I thought she might enjoy it, being around like-minded people.

ALICE. And I did. Mimi, I did enjoy it.

Pause. ELIZABETH *softens.*

ELIZABETH. Just tell me next time. So I know.

ALICE. I will.

ELIZABETH. And Mary, stop leading my little sister astray.

ALICE. I think you will find that it is the other way around.

ELIZABETH. Really?

MARY (*realising what* ALICE *means*). Oh the, yes, she has convinced me to join her and Frances on their next march.

ELIZABETH. Mary.

MARY. Thought I'd put these lungs to good use.

ELIZABETH. You are all insufferable.

ALICE. And yet you love us so.

ELIZABETH. That is because I am a disgustingly good person.

MARY. Miss Elizabeth Thompson, good? Surely not.

ALICE. I know. What a horrible thought.

They leave, laughing together.

THIRTY – BESSIE RA

1879. BESSIE *stands in front of* Remnants of an Army.

BESSIE. My dearest Elizabeth, you're back. With two
paintings. Two. Neither my favourite but that's not the point.
You've been nominated for associate Royal Academician.
You will be the first woman to ever be elected into the
academy. If you get in. Which you will. I knew, if anyone
was going to change stuff that it would be you. You're the
one that's gonna show us all how to do it. That it's possible.
And I'm not stupid, I know that I'm different to you, know
that it's gonna be harder for me. But everything in my life is
hard. Y'know, not having enough money and having to hide
my true self, I'm sure you understand. Well, actually, maybe
you don't, your life is quite different. (*Beat*.) I have thought
about offering myself up as a muse, y'know in exchange
for tuition, but I feel a bit strange about someone looking at
me, like that. Unless it was for you, I'd be a muse for you, if
you wanted? And then you could teach me to paint in return.
I can't afford paints yet but my drawings are good. Really
good, I think, I've come a long way since the dead dog. I try
and do what you do, y'know, pour all my emotions into it,
make it mean something, make it matter. I'm mostly angry
at the moment so they're all quite moody and broody. But
they're good, as good as most of these. Better than some.
Maybe you could have a look at them one day, when we
finally meet? Maybe when you're an RA you could make me
your protégée? Yeah and then you could nominate me for
membership. We'd be RAs together. We would make it the
best place in the world to be an artist. No, the best place in
the world to be a human. Write back to me and let me know
what you think.

THIRTY-ONE – THE VOTE

RA THREE *and* RA ONE *enter together.* MILLAIS *and* RA TWO *are waiting for them. They are at Burlington House.*

RA THREE (*to* RA ONE). Who nominated her?

MILLAIS. I did.

RA THREE. Of course.

MILLAIS. She deserves it.

RA THREE. Well, it will be you alone who votes for her.

MILLAIS. No, I don't think so.

RA THREE. Who? You stand alone / on this one.

RA TWO. Me.

RA ONE. You? But you hate women.

RA TWO. Well, yes. That is true. I do.

RA ONE. 'I'm not having a damned woman in.' You said that.

RA THREE. Yes you did, you literally said that. I heard you.

RA TWO. Well, I miss the feeling when she was around.

RA THREE. What feeling?

RA TWO. I do not know. But it was as though people thought I was good. I've never had that.

RA THREE. But you cannot be serious? You cannot actually want a woman in?

RA TWO. It might be worth it. I think, I think people actually quite liked me.

RA ONE *takes* MILLAIS *aside so the others can't hear.*

RA ONE. This is your fault.

MILLAIS. I merely nominated her. The men will vote as their hearts tell them to.

RA ONE. Their hearts? You believe that the men feel for this woman?

MILLAIS. I believe that they will do what is right.

RA ONE. You are a fool.

MILLAIS. Why are you so against it?

RA ONE. I do not have to explain myself to you.

MILLAIS. Are you frightened that the little women will usurp you?

RA ONE. Don't push it.

MILLAIS. Oh wait, you are.

RA ONE. You have no idea what you're doing. It all feels fun, a little naughty even, but you are messing with the natural order of things.

MILLAIS. Which is what? You at the top, running the art world?

RA ONE. Not everyone is suited to power.

MILLAIS. I agree.

RA ONE. I see what you are doing, Millais. Even if you cannot see it yourself.

MILLAIS. I am simply trying to change things for the better, move us all in a different direction.

RA ONE. Towards you, perhaps?

MILLAIS. No. Of course not.

RA ONE. But this new accepting academy will need a new man at the top. Out with the old.

MILLAIS. I am not doing this to get rid of you.

RA ONE. And yet where would I fit?

RA ONE *addresses the room before* MILLAIS *can answer him.*

Men. Gather, please, it is almost time to vote. But first I want to talk to you. (*Pause.*) What a world we live in. Things have changed so much, haven't they? And so quickly, I can hardly keep up. We have a nomination for a woman to join us within our innermost circle. A woman could be sitting here, right there, amongst all of you in a matter of days. That is no small thing. You all know that I believe it should happen, just not yet. I do not want us to be rushed, like the modern world would have us be. Move, move, move, make a decision, quick don't think. That is not us. I'm suggesting we vote no, for now, and then spend the next year really thinking about it.

MILLAIS. Another year? It has already been five years since the first calls for her election.

RA ONE. Yes, and we have come a long way. A woman has been nominated, thanks to you, Millais. She has had fame and success and a nomination. Quite a victory for women, really, in the past five years.

MILLAIS. We should vote her in.

RA ONE. Have you thought about the consequences? Because I have.

RA THREE. What consequences?

RA ONE. We vote her in. More and more women are inspired by her and believe that they can paint too. They send their pictures. Some of them are good. Better than yours. We have to hang them, it is only fair. But now there is not room for all of your paintings. (*To* RA THREE.) How many pictures did you submit this year?

RA THREE. Four.

RA ONE. And how many were accepted and hung?

RA THREE. Four. Three in Gallery Two.

RA ONE. Not if we let her in. You will be lucky if one is accepted. What with all the extra submissions we will receive from women.

MILLAIS. That is ridiculous.

RA ONE. Is it? There are other problems too, such as, who would escort her into dinner?

MILLAIS. What do you mean?

RA ONE. Well, she would not have a chaperone. Her husband cannot be here to lead her in. How would that work?

RA TWO. Blimey, it could not. Could it? No, I do not think it could work. Can it?

MILLAIS. No, there must be a solution.

They take a while to think, or not.

RA TWO. Do you know, I cannot think of one.

RA ONE. No. (*To* MILLAIS.) Can you?

MILLAIS. I'm not sure.

RA ONE. No, me neither.

MILLAIS. Do not let a technicality stop you from voting her in.

RA TWO. But she would not have a chaperone.

MILLAIS. Does that matter? Perhaps she does not need one.

RA TWO. Good God, man.

MILLAIS. These are modern thoughts but not completely outrageous.

RA THREE. But what if Uncle is right and there is not enough room for our work because of all the women?

RA TWO. I doubt that will happen /

MILLAIS. Thank you, some sense at last.

RA TWO. Most women's brains are too small for intellectual or creative pursuits. Lady Butler is an anomaly.

MILLAIS. No, no, that's not /

RA TWO. I will still vote for her. Perhaps she will not want to come to dinner.

RA THREE. Yes, my mother likes to stay at home of an evening.

RA TWO. It is a nice place for them to be. What with children and husbands and the like. I foresee that we hardly see her.

RA ONE. Is that a risk you are willing to take? Because I am not.

RA THREE. Oh, I don't know what to do. What should I do?

MILLAIS. You should make your own decision. Like a man. I trust that everyone will do what they believe to be right for the academy, and not just for themselves.

RA ONE. Yes, now we just need you to follow your own advice. (*Beat.*) Right, men, let's vote.

THIRTY-TWO – 'YOU ARE THE PROBLEM HERE'

It is the day of the vote. ELIZABETH *and* ALICE *are waiting at the academy.*

ALICE. You are nervous?

ELIZABETH. A little.

ALICE. It's going to be okay.

ELIZABETH. Yes.

ALICE. Elizabeth? I'm proud of you. (*Beat.*) Really, this is getting a bit ridiculous / surely they've voted by now.

ELIZABETH. Patience.

ALICE. Sorry. I just, it is just a little inconsiderate.

RA ONE, RA THREE *and* MILLAIS *enter.*

ELIZABETH. Here.

ALICE. Good luck.

RA ONE. You've been waiting.

ELIZABETH. Yes.

RA ONE. You needn't have. We would have sent a message. You would have been immeasurably more comfortable at home, I am sure.

ELIZABETH. I don't mind.

RA ONE. Clearly.

ALICE. Is there news?

RA THREE. The vote?

ALICE. Yes. Of course.

RA THREE. Yes.

ALICE. And?

ELIZABETH. Alice.

RA ONE. Alice? Ah yes, the sister infamous for her enthusiasm.

RA THREE. And poetry. This is the famous poet.

RA ONE. Yes, thank you.

ELIZABETH (*to* MILLAIS). You are quiet.

RA ONE. Isn't he?

MILLAIS. Elizabeth…

RA ONE. Lady Butler. Thank you for your nomination. It was so refreshing.

ELIZABETH. My pleasure.

RA ONE. But it was decided.

RA THREE. We are sorry to say.

RA ONE. We are so utterly sorry. We know this must come as a blow.

ALICE. Wait, what?

RA ONE. We're sorry.

ELIZABETH. I lost?

RA ONE. Yes. I know this must be hard to take, as a woman.

RA THREE. Since you could have been the first woman.

RA ONE. I can relate. I am a man with daughters.

RA THREE. And I a man with a mother.

ELIZABETH. What?

There's a horrifically awkward pause.

RA ONE. Yes. Well. Shall we?

RA THREE. Yes. Goodbye.

RA ONE. Farewell.

RA THREE. So long.

RA ONE. Adieu.

RA THREE. To you, and you, and you.

    RA ONE *and* RA THREE *leave.*

ELIZABETH. I lost.

MILLAIS. Elizabeth, I… I am sorry.

ELIZABETH. I lost?

ALICE. Yes.

MILLAIS. It was two votes.

ALICE. Two?

MILLAIS. Yes. Just two votes in it.

ALICE. She lost out by two votes only?

MILLAIS. I know it is a bitter disappointment but really,
    Elizabeth, really it could be seen as a victory.

ALICE. Don't.

MILLAIS. This is a positive thing for women.

ALICE. Don't you fucking dare.

ELIZABETH. No. It's fine.

ALICE. Mimi.

ELIZABETH. It's fine. It's fine. I'm fine.

> ELIZABETH *crumples into the background as the next scene swallows her up.*

THIRTY-THREE – 'A WOMAN WITHOUT A MAN IS LIKE A FISH WITHOUT A BICYCLE'

RA ONE, RA TWO, RA THREE *and* MILLAIS *are getting pissed.* MILLAIS *sits silently. During this scene the* RAS *and* MILLAIS *slowly become more real.*

RA TWO. Do you think she is gone?

RA ONE. Oh, yes.

RA TWO. Shame.

RA THREE. She seemed a little distraught. You could see it in her eyes. Dead. Empty.

MILLAIS. Hopeless.

RA TWO. Those eyes were so lovely and sparkly.

RA THREE. She really is very pretty still, for a woman her age.

RA ONE. Yes, not so young now.

RA TWO. Shame.

RA THREE. It is the way of the world.

RA ONE. I'd like to make a toast.

RA TWO. Magnificent.

RA THREE. Yes, do.

RA ONE. We, this veritable band of brothers, have made history today. We nearly, very, very nearly, elected a woman. A woman into the academy. What an achievement. I am immensely proud. Immensely. No one can say that we are not open to all. If you have the talent, and the determination then you can become an RA. Our doors are open. Our bloody windows are open too. We have succeeded. Many said we never would. That we were incapable of change. And yet, look. Look. Bloody look, men. We have. We nearly, very, very nearly let a damned woman in. And we have this man to thank for it.

RA ONE *drags* MILLAIS *forward*.

MILLAIS. No.

RA ONE. Yes. Yes. You are a good man.

MILLAIS. I failed.

RA ONE. But you came so close to succeeding. You're a man of the future. I am proud of you, and you should be proud of yourself. Proud of us. This 'liberal institution'.

MILLAIS. I truly believed that we were ready for change.

RA ONE. And we are. You have shown us that.

MILLAIS. But I lost. She is not an RA.

RA ONE. She is not. But you did not lose. You have bought us within two votes of having a woman in.This is a success for women. Men. This is a success for women.

MILLAIS. I suppose we have come a long way.

RA THREE. Yes.

RA TWO. I nearly let a damned woman in.

MILLAIS. Yes, I suppose.

RA THREE. Lads?

MILLAIS. Lads.

RA TWO *takes* RA ONE *aside*.

RA TWO. And now…

RA ONE. What do you mean?

RA TWO. When will the next one try? When will a damned woman actually become an RA? Next year, the year after?

RA ONE. Oh no, I'd say it will be a little longer than that. This is a guess, pulled from nowhere, utterly nonsensical, completely random. But it's going to be fifty-seven years.

THE RAS *slowly become* FRANCES, MARY, CORA *and* ALICE *under the next scene/song.*

THIRTY-FOUR – 'I'M A WOMAN PHENOMENALLY. PHENOMENAL WOMAN, THAT'S ME'

BESSIE *enters unnoticed by the others. They feel the weight of* ELIZABETH's *departure.*

BESSIE. What, you've given up? After everything. You've just, you've stopped. Fuck you. Fuck you. Like that's it, like we're finished. That's great, that's really great for you. Because you'll keep painting pictures and you won't need to strive for any more. You won't need to demand more. They've broken you. No, you let them break you. No door should have kept you out. You could have smashed it down, you could have burnt the whole thing to the ground. Opened every fucking door in the place, let us all in. But you wouldn't have, would you? If you'd become an RA nothing would have changed for me. It never does. Not for people like me. And I'm so tired, I'm so tired of things taking so long to change. One step forward and then always a shuffle back. There is no ending to this. It cannot end. That's, that's fucking exhausting. (*Pause.*) I don't think you've read any of my letters. And I don't think I want you to now. Farewell, I am, ever an admirer of your work. Bessie.

Song: 'Goodbye, Miss Thompson'

BESSIE.

> *Goodbye, Miss Thompson*
> *I am not sad to go*
> *I've wasted myself on you*
> *I could have been chasing a different dream*
> *And that stings, 'cause it's my fault*
> *It's my fault It's not about you.*
>
> *I'm tired and everything within me aches*
> *This heaviness is pulling me down*
>
> *I can't keep going on hope alone*
> *I'm going under, I'm going to drown*
>
> *Goodbye, Miss Thompson*
> *You can leave me alone*
> *I need so much more than you*
> *I should be searching myself for inner strength*
> *But fuck that, 'cause it's too hard*
> *It's too hard*
> *I need something new.*
>
> *I'm tired and everything within me aches*
> *This heaviness is pulling me down*
> *I can't keep going on hope alone*
> *I'm going under, I'm going to drown.*

The music continues as ELIZABETH, ALICE, FRANCES, MARY *and* CORA *gather together.*

FRANCES. Well? What happened?

ELIZABETH. The door has been closed.

MARY. What?

ELIZABETH. The door has been closed.

CORA. Elizabeth.

ELIZABETH. And wisely.

ELIZABETH *turns her back on them. She goes to leave.*

ALICE. No. Elizabeth.

> ELIZABETH *pauses, her heart breaks, she exits. The others all look to* ALICE.

No.

> BESSIE *continues singing.*

BESSIE.

> *I don't understand*
> *How I'm meant to keep up, keep, keep up*
>
> *I'm running and running and getting nowhere*
> *Everything hurts and I am going to fall, to fall*
> *And I can't stop thinking*
> *That wouldn't it be nice*
> *Really very nice*
> *Nice and pleasant*
> *To stop.*
>
> *I can see me lying, still as I wait*
> *A pretty little corpse, waiting for fate*
> *Waiting for someone to change their mind*
> *Realise they're wrong just in time*
> *But then I think of you*
> *And wake up, wake up, wake, up, wake up.*
>
> *So, goodbye, Miss Thompson*
> *I've got so much to do*
> *I've got so much life to live*
> *If I have to I'll do it all by myself*
> *I won't stop, when it's too tough*
> *I'm too tough*
> *It's me, it's not you.*
>
> *I'm tired and everything within me aches*
> *Sure heaviness is pulling me down*
> *But I'll keep going on hope alone*
> *I've got no choice, I've got no choice*
> *I won't let us drown.*

ALICE, FRANCES, MARY *and* CORA *talk in their group.*

BESSIE *sinks into the shadows, they listen.*

FRANCES. We need to persuade her that she's wrong.

ALICE. I do not think we can.

CORA. She is hurting, if we give her a little time.

MARY. I have never seen her like that.

ALICE. She has given up, understandably.

FRANCES. Is it? If Tennyson dies and you aren't given Poet Laureate, will you give up?

ALICE. No, I hope not. But after what has happened to Elizabeth I am under no illusion that it will actually happen.

MARY. Don't say that.

ALICE. I will hope for it, and fight for it but I have little faith that the Queen will choose me. If I am honest I do not see a woman being Poet Laureate for years to come. Possibly some strange futuristic year, like, twenty-oh-nine, or something.

CORA. That is horribly sad.

ALICE. That does not mean I have given up, that I will ever give up.

FRANCES. Good.

CORA. So, we keep going.

MARY. Yes, until the very end.

ALICE. It is going to be a long, long fight.

FRANCES. We know.

CORA. Where do we start?

ALICE. Do you know, I feel like burning some shit.

The others smile, unsure if ALICE *is joking.* BESSIE *steps out of the shadows.*

BESSIE. I have matches.

BESSIE *strikes a match.*

The End.

It's the end. Release the glitter.

Song: 'Bossy People'

ALL.
> *'Cause it's our time now*
> *It's our time*
> *Bossy people unite*
> *Bossy people it's time to fight.*
> *Fight – (Repeated.)*

A Nick Hern Book

Modest first published in Great Britain as a paperback original in 2023 by Nick Hern Books Limited, The Glasshouse, 49a Goldhawk Road, London W12 8QP, in association with Middle Child and Milk Presents

Cover photography by Jessica Zschorn; graphic design by Jamie Potter

Designed and typeset by Nick Hern Books, London
Printed in Great Britain by Mimeo Ltd, Huntingdon, Cambridgeshire PE29 6XX

A CIP catalogue record for this book is available from the British Library

ISBN 978 1 83904 232 4

www.nickhernbooks.co.uk

facebook.com/nickhernbooks

twitter.com/nickhernbooks